# Swans Through the House

George J. Farrah

Moria Books
Chicago, 2020

Copyright © 2020 by George J. Farrah

All rights reserved.

ISBN: 978-1-7337148-2-2

Moria Books
c/o Bill Allegrezza
9748 Redbud Rd
Munster, IN 46321

www.moriapoetry.com

Swans Through The House

|  |  | **BOOK** |
|---|---|---|
| **Many Eggs** | I | ... 1-12 |
| **Support Bones** | 11 | ... 13-19 |
| **Tiger** | III | ... 20-31 |
| **Catching Room** | IV | ... 32-101 |

Many Eggs

I

**Book 1.**

Or         the

enroll    of

abbots

using    t

he     star     adz

of    the    factory      stack

that     lives or     one

year   only       atavistic

he deftly          handles    the lever

bashful          the city         sinks

to where

it was found

bit map

 of behaviors               oceans

       brain     wave    of         brass

**Book 2.**

A carrion of caboodle in the casein cajoling

it would even out in the horizon caution

believe it would be a prize of old cider trees

column of colonies eat their way as light givers

in front of the court of colors

a dab fish a cytology a dachshund I am their pet

a daisy damaged by a dairy

a deport of intentions strung like a tent

a dislocation of water instead of always speaking

of cane the dressage of the nations bespeaks advertising

**Book 3.**

An elephant   is

                        an   elevate

etch   or

 euro

                 smoke

                         changing

fanny   family   fly   erodes

                    a flare

                       occurs

a   free

frankincense               freemason

the

language

                       of pens

in   our   words

            a   grape   vine

        through

    granite our   town

                 a   handcuff   hallucination

he says

a hill powered

the    hypocritical    consciousness

retires

**Book 4.**

Reasons

  incontinently    increase

  interface of the face

    o

  well I tried


jogtrot jive jodhpur jewels


  a lamping speaks quickly here


a small

    primary

             personal interests

    lurch the

    luster of having it

masticating mats clean shoes

he speaks

  in millibars

             she speaks

    with motion

## Book 5.

The  nest  of the arm or

observe   the deep sea of sky

   outgrow armored wings and sink

   paroxysm of masters  over

peruse   with primates

plausible conferences  bored   and disband

exactly like confusion  yet

the property of the world belongs to that word so

  says the world

as others sleep

**Book 6.**

The   rack   of wind
  unhooked with reeds
resurface
    that thought


routines thicken around him
 scald the wounds
   of the scalding
   self-respect that rests
 un-provable but
   to direct it speaking up drafts
   the smarming encounter
speedwell   slowness of blue growth
   the stationers of the city
                    the strontium
                gales of walls

## Book 7.

Swaggering   the clouds  of her   browse
teak team over t
             he falling
right at the threshold of   liberty lies flourish
as the whole
        desert scene totters
             a trowel of a smile
           ruling for measure
       the urine of the pines
volt-face but popular
         welded and preserved   talking freely
twisted hair of feet
the zilch of zombies    no zwieback

**Book 8.**

The
ability not to choose
   acid forms of knowledge
  the affixing o f friendships
the
other road
 pines friendship
building
  attached
 to memory
   blue green studying the stars
housed personnel making ink
   bigmouth teeth over the hedge
brawl with his hair split out
  a spearing buffer budding
putting a block of soap into the cage
  a car a bird a paper a motor

# Book 9.

Causeway of
    particulars  general seed
  a car of support and casual friendly
muscular group   a ring of swimming plants
a cloth of  or  piece of   bent wire
    the colonnade of jello to move backbone
the controller of more elements
a music and well in order the other receives goods


  a cool propellant water birds
      the cake of love to frighten a cowboy
    a crummy container for salt arrives
    the yellow with   to criticize a dairy
the deep freeze characterizations medals pleasant
  to make a place like a crane
  to diffuse digital watches in your mind


  the ticket of disorganization dislodges
frightened dregs  drill needed defense  which floats
a rarity inn an eager way not high ranking noblemen

**Book 10.**

An eagle of an earned kites
  nothing electrify
an enroute dream
  (the original negative)
even a flattened
    strawberries
  expert
am in love with
a fiber
 and sleep
flagstone combination
      a catch the bus picture
        the money in France

**Book 11.**

Furtive

                        land      slides   in a     fuse
box
the    entire    genetic    library
the   glory  of  the  glossy  cupboard   room
the    horizontal    graffiti   piano
the   hologram  of   the   famous   hamlet
which   are    pieces   of    clo
th
the    lander   in    high    season
bitter    glass   of     crowds

**Book12.**

The hoof of the blue sky
      to form
      relevant
items
an        imperative of    talking
being a    defiant
 result
informal violence of the sun
      the intelligence    settles to the feet
the ire of colony made  him

Support Bones

II

**Book 13.**

                                            To throw humorous

a kilo of radio waves

                  a languid laser surrounded by land

                          outside planting trees

      start a flat narrow skiers to lighten luggage

  a locket of locomotion

                  a lurid amount abundantly

   a manacle of chess

                     mastoids filled with pleasure

getting better pre-historic people

**Book 14.**

A gesture used

a mock mediator of candy

a wall plant uses mouths anyway

a tropical agreement into a tent

tubes of the opponent

facing knotted from

my lens morally obliged to help

**Book 15.**

The onto

                        onset is open again

ought expressing

                        outgrew metallurgical

things

the trousers worn in bed

the science showing you feel bad

a small what you want   of there forms

the concrete

                        shelters

                        stitched to   your hand

a plant  iron   vertical amusing

hair

                        understood by most people

from them   everywhere matters

anindividualinnewspapersmagazines

**Book 16.**

A future search protean defenses

a purpose press your lips     the sky (Jimmy)

a horse estimates a passage

ready

 just the lines

                         on a hand

from a small fort to a tall look

then later a close carelessness and meeting

**Book 17.**

The plausible possible musicale instrument
    (The plectrum of desire)
in poppy of his eye  the takes you
  a prefab quantity of rain and snow
  an armed ship of former individuals
    a medicine which is sold for the court
    a puppet which moves his cynicism
    a common wild animal is rare
    a black bird ready to wear  has an answer
 the re-echo of plashing

**Book 18.**

To rend the announcement into trees

a restore of eyes and fingers a retrospect

the rigor of the hand testing the wind

the beautiful ruble of clouds from where this is not hidden

the wild trains growing in the water

with x-ray sharpened flowers

**Book 19.**

A survey of sand under my bare feet

a half conscious glass of water

and over a shamble the well rises

which shakes the medicines

the bash to move physical properties

making a hissing sound as a state of being

"a special trustworthy military is hard to find"

the speck of justice who spells his life

a sudden small pigeon over the fairy ears

a static of enough flood

the stamp is a company

to follow ones cows costs

stubble and technique

Tiger

III

**Book 20.**

A stone of sky or water

                        the stuff stuck on his shoe again

the sun of traffic calculated

a shoulder at the start of things

                        a tag at dusk raises wonderful

ghosts and shouts


a cozy tear gas kind of day

                        an animal bird visited in an area by

traveling salesmen

a part of your neck below the crowd

**Book 21.**


A picture of property he was
    a tough paper for it
    shape of the pass


a truck of the dreams and soldiers
    a two stroke duck in his brain
    undercoat  a clothes line of water


an unpack lifts the moon

    a house   an usher to the town

**Book 22.**

Verify the verse is at an angle

      the bitter sound of a vocational diamond

in the washbowl  dead  flies

   well founded levitation over the fire

these sticks and wild birds

      a woozy amount of wool problems

  yum yum two oxen on a cliff

## Book 23.

Abutted the commercial rolls down
   parking brakes
the acrylic parking lot forbids
                  a battlefields' letters
the job of years applies
      forward to a thin film
an alm of it he pointed
       the gun to agriculture
the tree which often grows
  either right or the morning
the presenter dislikes truth
   answering addiction each year
asking for a desire to eat
arms linked
   something is laid out
a lovers meeting rhymes using vowels only

**Book 24.**

The astringent mono atoms of your smile

avid weights banned on this canoe

badgering the hearts of these wilderness bailiffs

a noise made by so many things

a beaming of all of their between the pillars

besieged latter remembering all of this better than anyone

and a birch in the place of ones birth

**Book 25.**

The blowzy crowd   he hid in him

a bongo of her hi bone cheek

a box of

                shoulders but no opponent anywhere

a brim of brightness

                a small country I met by chance

a machine of a local road

a person who eats

they were playing cards

Book 26.

The eye action of catching rooms in ancient times

a certain

        middle in the distance

the chemical eyes    protect the king

a chop of a

            ballet person

a level with a black board    now a screen

    a cloudy coal club

the coke collects in fibers like tissue

an occasion

to steer troops into college

**Book 27.**

A closet of shovels and clots

in the warm collecting windows

   a remark happens to be representative

and compresses the compliments which helps

sweets and cakes   paper   thrown   proving wrong

a marriage a pattern in the sky citizens

**Book 28.**

oil and water as thought and thinking

as being and movement mode and mood

a convention conveyer

corn of corduroy

a bed wetside becomes our galaxy

in different calculations and tax

edible tenfooted insurance

a very pale in a craft for memory

**Book 29.**

The cunning of clouds

a damage in the upper part of it

a link through decals and bone and words

the deftness with trees easily damaged

to depend on cotton in a fire

the dial of color not straight forward

**Book 30.**

A diminished camera

a discretion above


the distill effort of games

a dome of dollars


where there is only one

    a beard of tax falls from the bridge

   the drogue of issues

here makes a water proof

the unfriendly kid sitting on the edit

in order to embark and ellipse the ignore

## Book 31.

The fine stated elsewhere and complete

to entwine and wade into principal

a seashore shapes his feet

leaves and theories ways of walking

making fingers explicable

a small tiredness in the eyes

a fastener of distant farmers

the sense of the responsible foot

Catching Room

IV

## Book 32.

Caring pumps involving lights
a flannel leg up to therefore
preventing   by moving soft pieces
in more weather than a ship
weeds break into small pieces
a street of frivolous aching stones
  advancing the computer becomes distant
a length sent out by radio active gambles
  people of wool link with strong gloves
thin hands overcome old age
a forgiving frame of trees

**Book 33.**

At the forum formula walls/towers

a hiding Freud seems to show

but another which frequently toes

the fox from the well a fragile

a friend gives out a frog as a reminder

cave and attention to its welcoming fuzzy logic

## Book 34.

The gantry of his childhood

a transparent

small summer house

the positive against the avalanche

the geyser  of light   the geyser

  the pleasure

      of temporary blindness

he understands the gravel may hurt

    a growl of the crowd as an important person

the hair of visitor smells so good

**Book 35.**

A handrail over the reasoning

hangman by a hangnail

clearing the haven't finally

a hello from the hedonists no anger

how the earth by common water bird we said

   a side of the fire all over the place gratefully

a hopscotch and a public teenage dancing

bad tempered once what changed it?

   the lambs hypochondria was understandable


immersed as an immobile lighting

as painters trying to transform themselves

**Book 36.**

The incorporate lips of her
  induce the intelligible dissolve
the inhale of ingress music's

**Book 37.**

The instability instinct

the questioning cut across each other

iridescent with iron

jamboree cows

ability to see things


a settlement of force

  clumsy poisonous seeds

lapwig laser calls

  to do nothing against good else

**Book 38.**

Being thin

to loose hold rising in the air

calcium deposits and green color

bedding of straw

and not very exact

but the lull is wonderful

keeping the postal service

a manifold presence of winking eyes

referring to an afternoons play manual

a melody of temperature in cycles per second

to gibe a well metaphysics

a country to another

**Book 39.**

Fat and water fed
  referred by shepherds
a special instrument
street or group of streets
  closed to traffic
 the action mirrors
  such as  printers

**Book 40.**

A pile drivers

the pivot of alternative fingers

the plunder as often

a common flower in quite a bad way

sometimes genetic conventions

building in advance before you

**Book 41.**

To tell the truth is happening
 before a war person who has admiration
admiration takes privacy

things which assumed claim possession
 daintily the king prevaricates then you are
not to tell the truth pressurize the performance
who maybe displaced before noticed
a pre war council of prey is true that
certain conditions make this possible at all

**Book 42.**

Rehearse again for great happiness

in the new house or apartment

to spread the risk of a normal life

a relapse of reindeer members of the family

a strap which controls metal rods

new soldiers quit and support others more or less

"a strong regular interval doesn't make up for wrong"

he said

"a child's progress in school reopens a person"

she said

**Book 43.**

A rust belt of action

for three days a small person

  his noise is coming nose running

a school of plant I have decided

from one column of dry leaves/silk

standing free form in the dusk

a new engine slowly until it works properly

**Book 44.**


With a projection part

a line payment a line of battle

a period of time pariahs of public bar

wild animals sandblast shoes

a tapestry panel of birds and animals

scent from this truce

nevertheless a small Chinese boat


between the oranges and hillside

makes crimped connections into plugins

boiling water for tea under the bridge

**Book 45.**

A person who saws or saves wood
  a scrap of scramble can make you
to agree and along the edge of the sea
  another self portrait
separate from a large country
in the center of a building
  a shoelace hooves
dawn legs seeing the sights
  boy part of a device gripping
full of cigarette smoke and waiting
  a dissolve solidifying
to put seeds into the earth

**Book 46.**


a metal plant protected

   spurn of small quantities

a person who is paid


the diver


connects    with the original shape

a stampede

               of formality

enclose in life a letter

the company

 rising   from   the

                 floor of a cave

carpet

 in place with air or water

a long   rubber   stamp on the

                       round

flight of stairs full of stars

**Book 47.**

The steam which comes form engines
to prevent the air from turning into shadows


a stream of gnats because of sun
subconscious a speech blocks motion of persons
a soft leather who dwells   successively away

# Book 48.

The gratitude in forms
    the neck
  complete
        a peg used
    as an oarlock
through thunder another persons
a pointed place and a small bird
your system of writing your name
the paper broken over a leg
  no two sides parallel to the equator
water seam shock turn the å
one bad your thumb around and around
the mad beaten controlled unbounded
  undress the unfastened calm
and movements to other people
the air around the uvula

**Book 49.**

The velocity of anxiety
  pumps in fresh air
who surface like velvet
to cover with a heart

when you consider a vile way
  referring to reign of the king or queen
the psychological impact of their victims
strong conference between small windows
the particular jobs
telephones with your voice

**Book 50.**

A thunder bolt of reasons

a clock witch or lock

thick cloth for everything

a paper showing illegally

an airplane laughing through

you can remove tight steps

expanding dreams fro a minuet

cover the floor and walls

**Book 51.**

The tilt of the tips

and part of water

teach us Lord

information ringing

like a bird in the chest

boundaries to make us wary

a title of the angry speech

the tin rattles asleep

the hourly medicine disclosed

**Book 52.**

Your teeth with shame

a system of the upper body

large circus feet

a torrent which you can hold$\pi$

to make reveal

a flaming piece of wood

common brown and red butterfly

**Book 53.**

The waning wanderlust returned
  in a full watered waterfall like a dog
a strong sport such a lifting
  to stop tour bait the crowd
the wind crunches by moving the face
    to ask yourself to be alone for awhile

**Book 54.**

Worsted wow twisting movement

to fight with line of meaning

  which has brokeninto rest

a road engine asleep and sounding

a secrete might look poor in this light

**Book 55.**

The yo yo yowl

over the naked chest

young when pressed

a dress of his language

**Book 56.**

An abide which waves

to   remove   or

                                          carry in this

the comments latest development

a grinding way of speaking

if they consider it a useless peculiarity

helpless

                    another

            persons musical instrument

a soloist of bellows a bag charged sharper

the ability to carry sound with distortion

**Book 57.**

The admission moves until one is changed slightly

and to talk to a person who is next

showing admiration

a card when flying

the air made to stir a wing

## Book 58.


    To

            pretend

to

             policy

                     airplane

a written statement to a larger one


to

fill

                stir

                     with

air

a person around the earth

**Book 59.**

A head the attacking minor

help instrument immune

mirror illness

travel by

the past

to make it worse

then to agree with

**Book 60.**

Drinking tiny water plants

in a there substance soft drink

obey him referring to allegory

worn out to be everything everyone

two possible meanings

a general area piles up

in the natural mineral salt

a condition a particular shape

medical temperature returns

and in a fortune of turns

yellow orange low gardens

very well done

made of fossilized resin

**Book 61.**

An anarchy holds logs in the hearth

a very large snake  occurs

with close examination a substance which

contains liquid for the eyes

ships which can anchor as a drug

the machine which amplifies

**Book 62.**

Annual that you may become fat

event in the past

which comes before

anorak is a jacket with a hood he told me

over the telephone

                                    to give you an appetite

the opposite block saying you are sorry

**Book 63.**

The fitness referring to

  which lives in water

to go near rough argonrmal

showing wet roofs  based on theory

a part of your decision to stop fighting temporarily

a person who studies astronomy

sports where your run making amends

**Book 64.**

Auricle of Australia

her hand

  the back of my mind

stumps in the crickets

balaclava simply for decoration

blew snow into instruments

and assets of a bantamweight

the compound forecasting the weather

**Book 65.**

A small ointment through the 70's

a beagle a bean the end on a rifle


which projects form  an outside wall

very quick feel for it mouth

a large fierce woman transmitted per second


monaural rude invasion from coffee

a person who sleeps in the same bed

bees producing beer and berries

hopes mattress pillows

**Book 66.**

    A beneficent

people making dots

bestir quite mad

  which is always present

who becomes a doctor

    betwixt every two years

a strip of wood

    to claim a book

**Book 67.**

Arrows plant

                                      with purple or bottles

bodies forward having a wide road

with legs curve like a butterfly

a container with wild blackberry

identification putting on the breaks

**Book 68.**

I was born who breeds
       path for a year
separated like the color of wood or soil
soap and barley husband or wife
  slight shock from biting


underground quantities of a town
where it flowers in spring
over a dividing wall
small finch and a foolish action

**Book 69.**

A burst or measure of grain

underwater message sent to a stove pipe

put on skin to smooth

a noisy hill by a cable

benefiting from two quite opposite things

a man who operates a movie of white flowers

keeping a large valley

caressing the heart

clappers made of history or a machine which

operates recordings or drawers

a swollen ear

endless metal belt running

to ask a question

an entertainer

a cavemen

plant a flower

and

readonlymemory

**Book 70.**

A certain measure of length or tasks

condemnation to compare central maneuvers

gunpowder and soup and change two seas


to bring at a tufted surface and an opponent

chinks in the chlorine fence diary of an American animal

cider making motion pictures around a church


a bell which strikes in your hand mind noisy hinged shell

**Book 71.**

Which shows pink flowers

                        are necessary cards

in the code of the origin of a room

praiseworthy a collage of police


you can not compare them

           referring to concepts and a strange treaty

**Book 72.**

The confounding conformation

an honor to be under it

and elsewhere unions and small pieces


to a point to be made

and an admission of fault

the mountains make that firm

as do keyboards armed

a care to trust your deeper interest


a person who feels music

and then consigns old building to thought

**Book 73.**

Knowledge with whom you're contacted

restraining the same dates

coffee rolls or bread

near a heater which warms

a chord is printed in an apple

a flirtatious type of explosive

a motion picture housing people

the magazine is edible and combines

risk with disaster as if to row a boat

**Book 74.**


The crayon in the crease
   where to make an invent
the ground which climbs up a wall
    to believe and promise to walk through


      a rolled variety in an ankle for support

**Book 75.**

The crusade again to paint them

  a sugar of non metric shapes

a clock where cryogenics

as a number multiplied

implanted cuddled given number

of animals and painter is used


the capacity and a person from Cuba

a cellar or under a church

**Book 76.**


a curlew under the skin

      wraps a curve of custard

eats the natural waves twist

  a spot of light which

inside like a Dalmatian

dad by building and intents

small pink and white

the character of a wheel

  davenport for the new car

to make glasses falling  into ruin

**Book 77.**

To declare it   deciduous deck

mind form of the different cases of wind

going slower out of code moves

    which postponement form holy orders

defusing the trees

who forms  part of crowd

a demented job an important job

## Book 78.

Demolishing and appealing many people want it

forming like a sea

who on the direct route to discover noise

  is pronounced in the ground for planting

I love a cup of surface

angels in the engines a devil on my mind

  make it weather which dims a light

**Book 79.**

The disc
  of discipline
the normal price
water which has been used
 hiding one persons
we will have to accept paper
 being dominant in Oxford
gloom form wood   in which dolls can be cut
evacuating the North Atlantic for a the dress

**Book 80.**

Dropped off in    the   medicine    count
to call a drop
    kick a
large falloff
dark and a small  shore bird


   the ground letter working clothes
a person who owns sandy ridges by thethe sea
who is this dry surface covered with dust
what ever made you say that

**Book 81.**

Paths toward the east

high spirits   chocolate or sugar

one of the points of a wall


"educated" the radio to speak

       a coil of information

heater stove made by a beating heart

**Book 82.**


A quarrel into parts

color   of this stone

each as fire

to raise the cold   patterns of sowing

a physical expression

 a way of playing

who shows a whole plan

balanced the points of wearing away

erasure of the real adventure

which very little has been engraved


as an example an animal carries away fumes

  pipe in a car rule or law runs the business

exhume material like gunpowder

in a direction of a man who was the armed service

as a small look into house

and private sprouts into his victory head

the nation fully transparent and threateningly anonymous

**Book 83.**


The    stand    in    line
falsely being with white spots


draped and very hungry
father fatigue he is leading


most people think terror casing weak points
to   try
    to get in is
usually image sent by telephone
   which    produces   gov.   felons
(small figures wanting so much war)


filled with   chemicals   or foam to put out
friendly    with fish spoken in Finland
refusing to change
             the end of your fingers
  a flash back down
               like a birds wing

**Book 84.**

Referring to sex

which carries goods or people

a wheel with seats

leaves of salt

rope mat

stooping coal

protecting

thigh bone

**Book 85.**

The fidgety field

in the glasses

then it makes sense

the center of the firmament

info close at hand

**Book 86.**

A filament of the firmament
    to make pipes or wheels
a flashbulb collapses with tiredness
you can attach pieces of cork when you walk
a larger slice of ice with tow wings
constant turns a flood of flirts
which makes a deep loud sound
arms of foam folk people
traditional stories
water as it moves

**Book 87.**

The format against the enemy

left in a rock

release from a difficult situation

   having no friends holes in a funeral

galloping in the highest rows cheapest seats

gardens of sharp intakes of breath

and a plant whose bulbs

superior military poses

recovering from a long illness

**Book 88.**

To receive around a corner
get up get off lightly
  birth rumored fighting the reader
too old for speech by phone
      more appealing with no contents
to look briefly the shadow turns
to go first bright flower spikes
  without asking for any
smooth no hair referring to ice
in an arena of trees
    frequently in the window of a church
clouds in Mean Time Fishing

**Book 89.**

The  to keep erotic

trumpet shaped flowers

to become an article of clothing

 like a section of skirt

shaped like a triangle

their relationship in language

 I admit speaking is marked on I

growing as stars clustered

in the ditch in soap on a bed

**Book 90.**

Great Granddaughter

Great Grandson

referring to cooked green vegetables

does not break

the profit of plumage

a stare of welcome

green stick fracture

the land covered

he took to melted animal fat

**Book 91.**

Aquatinted with a crowd of pleasant sounds

who repairing sleep with a restaurant

wooden bone houses

spaces between threads of a vet

stables processing micro chips

the first floor of a person

water mixed with apples

a soft earth changes pitch

**Book 92.**


The guest speaking in the cold

  a quilt of missiles loud course laughs

sacrifice to business where people

a small village hammers their belongings

diamond patterned clouds

**Book 93.**

A company of fire

in stems and hands

    haunting a game of tennis

the evening of the huge field

in the dust of voices and

trees of stars


 and a person who drinks

from very hot weather

**Book 94.**

The ports of iron caring oxygen
  planted with yourself like plans
sewn edge of the earth
  not important floors
to attach to the legs of a horse
domestic words used by your magicians
acclimating to small doses of a dangerous drug
  a humble hue use for sailing
which skims over the water on their legs

**Book 95.**

A harp blade is a peculiar pursuer

achieving  an ideal as others

to mark i

diomatic summers

some months of memory

which identifies the holder

you have the same ice floating or not

a picture of Christ or a symbol on a computer

a 'difficult' person a being  about to happen and change

sudden intractable details with a smile

**Book 96.**

With which you need agree
  be comforted
in an incompetent way
in a way which does not make sense
excluding certain groups of people
being incompatible in thought
not to be compared
incompletely
 falsely imagining
not thinking of other people
when their language
without a definite result
for a book of hot weather in Autumn

**Book 97.**

One main cannot live not thinking

                false fit calls lack of who cannot

statistics from slight living

careless about the body

food pain in love poems fireplace


not be imitated but of course

the glorious pressure

within which you cannot understand

Book 98.

Sound escaping
in an intelligent way
  insulating material
microchip not obeying
a musical note
touch which cannot be born
touch which cannot be defined
in one piece understood and loved
recently rooms in a ship from time to time


                cut
speech
into networks
attack music sung at the beginning of church
the law
   cannot be found again
so they say patterns of grammar
   the condition of pain integrity and hope

**Book 99.**

A box in which Jerusalem comes from
  to
aim for
   the bluish green color of jade
outer ease of covering a cover for a book
   the high mutiny boot with jade underfoot
stones worked triangular sail in front
up form the elbow at an easy pace
pouring liquids into a person who juggles
a nipple in keeping because

**Book 100.**

Card of others friend

a tendency to steel supplies while

breathing into a persons mouth

being kind

bird of light wood

**Book 101.**

Which leads to a loss patience

the earth's sufferance

at the end of a list

with a rope and a theory


of hot milk and pages and 3 miles

 a hate which flowers  and electric wire

the purpose of entering as a new born

without any numbers a legend of walking

long green grace

machines dissolve balls of pink fire

**George J. Farrah** holds an MFA from Bard College, The Milton Avery School of Fine Arts, NY. He has published two full-length books of poetry with Ravenna Press: *The Low Pouring Stars* and *Relieved of Their Whispers* (forthcoming). With Locofo Chaps, he has published *Walking as a Wrinkle, 100 Days of Protest, a* chapbook. His other works include *Insomniac Plum*, a chapbook, *This Space for Correspondence,* an anthology including poetry and visual work, and *Triple No. 10*, an anthology including his drawings and the work of two other writers, all from Ravenna. He is also a painter, exhibiting nationally, with work in both private and corporate collections, represented by Douglas Flanders and Associates. His paintings can be found on the Douglas Flanders website and on his professional site, gjfarrah.com.

**Books/E-Books Available from Moria Books**

Jordan Stempleman's *Their Fields* (2005)
Donna Kuhn's *Not Having an Idea* (2005)
Eileen R. Tabios's *Post Bling Bling* (2005)
Anny Ballardini's *Opening and Closing Numbers* (2005)
Garin Cycholl's *Nightbirds* (2006)
lars palm's *Mindfulness* (2006)
Mark Young's *from Series Magritte* (2006)
Francis Raven's *Cooking with Organizational Structures* (2006)
Raymond Bianchi's *American Master* (2006)
Clayton Couch's *Letters of Resignation* (2006)
Thomas Fink's *No Appointment Necessary* (2006) Catherine Daly's *Paper Craft* (2006)
Amy Trussell's *Meteorite Dealers* (2007)
Charles A. Perrone's *Six Seven* (2008)
Charles Freeland's *Furiant, Not Polka* (2008)
Mark Young's *More from Series Magritte* (2009)
Ed Baker's *Goodnight* (2009)
David Huntsperger's *Postindustrial Folktales* (2010) Gautam Verma's *The Opacity of Frosted Glass* (2011)
rob mclennan's *Kate Street* (2011)
Garin Cycholl's *The Bonegatherer* (2011)
j/j hastain's *autobiography of my gender* (2011)
Kristina Marie Darling's *narrative (dis)continuities: prose experiments by younger american writers* (2013)
Jay Besemer's *A New Territory Sought* (2013)
Joel Chace's *One Web* (2014)
Garin Cycholl's *Horse Country* (2014)
Eileen Tabios' *I Forgot Light Burns* (2015)
lars palm's *look who's singing* (2015)
Ed Baker's *Neighbor* (2015)
Tom Beckett's *Appearances: A Novel in* Fragments (2015)

Charles Perrone's *Out of Alphabetical Order* (2015)
Piotr Gwiazda's *Aspects of Strangers* (2015)
Freke Räihä's *[title missing] –a quality of motion* (2016)
Kristian Carlsson's *A Crack at the Origins* (2016)
Matina L. Stamatakis' *A Late Sketch of Final Doves* (2017)
Mark Young's *The Perfume of the Abyss* (2019)
Lopez's, Bloomberg-Rissman's, and Marshall's *The End of the World Project* (2019)
Joel Chace's *Threnodies* (2019)
George J. Farrah's *Swans Through the House* (2020)

The e-books/books can be found at www.moriapoetry.com

www.ingramcontent.com/pod-product-compliance
Lightning Source LLC
Chambersburg PA
CBHW031407040426
42444CB00005B/446